Y0-FPI-893

A READY-TO-READ BOOK

the hippopotamus

by BOBBI HERNE
illustrated by JEANNE HUNT MILLER

Consultants

HAROLD J. TANYZER, PH.D., Hofstra University
ALBERT J. MAZURKIEWICZ, ED.D., Newark State College

WONDER BOOKS • NEW YORK
A Division of GROSSET & DUNLAP, Inc.

This popularly priced edition is a reprint in the traditional alphabet of a book originally published for schools in Pitman's Initial Teaching Alphabet.

Copyright © 1965

Initial Teaching Alphabet Publications, Inc.
Publishers of Educational Materials in Pitman's Initial Teaching Alphabet
20 East 46 Street, New York City, N.Y. 10017

All rights reserved. No part of this book may be reproduced
in any form without the written permission of the publisher.

Printed in the United States of America

1-987654321

Once upon a time, the hippopotamus lived on the land. Next to the elephant, he was the largest of all the animals. Second Largest of the Animals is what the other animals called him.

The animals called him this because they didn't know his real name. He wouldn't tell them his real name. He was very ashamed of it because it was big and clumsy, just as he was. He could hardly move, and he could hardly say his name — Hippopotamus.

He never moved from the shade of the big breezy tree. This was the only cool place in all the land. And Hippo was so big that he took up most of the shade. Even there he was hot and sticky all the time. His skin was very thick and heavy.

Mr. Hippopotamus had a very thoughtful wife. She was big and clumsy, too. But every day she would walk to the river to get some water. Then she would sprinkle it on him. This made him cooler. But it made her hotter. So she would collapse under the big breezy tree. Then all the shade was used up by Mr. and Mrs. Hippopotamus. The other animals had no cool place to go.

Something had to be done, of course. The other animals thought and thought. Finally they thought of a marvelous plan. If the Second Largest of the Animals lived in the water all the time, he would always be cool. If the Second Largest of the Animals lived in the water all the time, his wife would not collapse from the heat. And if the Second Largest of the Animals lived in the water all the time, there would be enough shade for the other animals. And they told him.

But Hippo was big and clumsy. He just wouldn't move, even though the other animals tried to make him move.

He knew that no one but his wife knew his name, so he said to them, "If you can guess my name, I will move to the water."

Then the animals began to guess.
"Gerion," said the rabbit.
"No," said the hippopotamus.

"Hyelephant," said the zebra.
"Wrong!" said the hippopotamus.

"Is your name Tiglet?" asked the deer.

"Wrong again." He knew no one would ever guess Hippopotamus.

One by one the animals began to leave — all except the turtle. He drew himself into his shell. He thought and thought.

The next day the turtle went down the path that Mrs. Hippo took to the river. He dug a hole in the path and hid in it. The hole was just deep enough so that the top of his shell was level with the ground. When the turtle was in the hole, his shell looked like a smooth stone.

Soon he felt the very heavy foot
of Mrs. Hippopotamus on his back.
The turtle jumped.

"Oh! Oh!" cried Mrs. Hippopotamus. "Help! I have stumbled on this stone. Help me, Hippopotamus."

"Aha!" thought the turtle. Once more he lay still. Once more he looked like a stone.

On the next day, all the animals gathered once more around the hippopotamus. Once more they began to guess his name.

"Kangelot."

"No."

"Snork."

"No."

"Ostron."

"No."

The animals were very discouraged. But the turtle called, “Wait! I know his name. His name is Hippopotamus!”

And the Second Largest Animal grunted, "Yes." He knew he had to keep his word. The other animals gathered in the shade of the big breezy tree. They watched the hippopotamus walk slowly to the river with his wife.

Just as the other animals thought, Mr. and Mrs. Hippopotamus were happier there. To this day, the river is where they live. And the other animals were happier too, under the shade of the big breezy tree.